Microwave Dreams

Microwave Dreams

You can't skip the process, but you can speed it up. Making your dreams come true faster.

Jeremy Boykin

Cover design by Edwin Cuen

ISBN-13: 9781794668614

Printed in the United States

Thank you, God, for saving my life. I love you with all my heart. And to my family & friends who are always just one phone call away, I wouldn't be here without you.

Table of Contents

INTRO

D ear Dreamer,

The struggle is real. Trust me I know! I've made a lot of mistakes, taken a lot of entrepreneurial risks, & have failed miserably several times. I've had more things go wrong than right in my life. Although I've experienced a lot of failure and pain, I wouldn't change any of it because without it, I wouldn't be able to inspire YOU! Since I just admitted to you that I've failed quite a bit, you're probably wondering what makes me qualified to write a book. Well, maybe it's because I've traveled within the US to speak for thousands of dollars. Or maybe it's because my clothing brand, GOD IS THE PLUG, has been in over 65+ stores across the country. Or maybe it's because I've survived over 6 car accidents, a tornado, and a cancer scare without a scratch. Or maybe, simply put, I'VE HAD SOME OF MY DREAMS COME TRUE. Despite the countless roadblocks I've faced throughout my life,

<u>from serious financial struggles to trusting the wrong people, my dreams have come true...and I'm still dreaming.</u>

If I'm honest with you, I know A LOT about life. Life and I have been battling it out since birth. But it seems like no matter what I go through MY DREAMS NEVER DIE! Do you have any dreams that seem to never die? Personally, I am a bonafide dreamer: "Hi, my name is Jeremy & I am addicted to dream chasing." I'm always going after some dream of mine, hence why I fail a lot. If you take a lot of shots, you're bound to miss a lot of shots, but you can never make the shots you're not willing to take. So, I just keep on shooting. In today's society, we are constantly seeking knowledge from those who have had massive amounts of success, whether they've taken a lot of shots or not. Meanwhile, I see the phrase "failure is the best teacher" stamped all over everyone's social media. It doesn't say success is the best teacher, it says FAILURE! If that's the case, then I am 100% qualified to help in making your dreams come true.

Throughout my roller coaster journey as a business owner and inspirational speaker, I've learned more than I could put on a shirt or in a speech. So, I decided to write a book! You may be thinking, "there is no way I can relate to you because we work in different industries," But I have experience in several industries including hospitality, e-commerce, brick and mortar, fast food, retail, entrepreneurship, clothing design, YouTubing, social media marketing, event coordinating, public speaking, music artistry, sales, website design, professional college student (lol), and so much more! Yeah, I've done a lot so far in my 30-year-old life. I can't even lie, by now I expected to be a millionaire, yet I'm nowhere near it. My desire for instant success played a huge role in many of my failures. What if I told you I could scratch that anxious itch you've been having for success? What if I told you I could help you achieve your dreams faster than you could ever imagine? What if I told you I had some special information that could transform your entire life? It doesn't matter if you are happy, sad, lonely, or depressed, I have the remedy that you're seeking!

You're probably thinking, "yeah, I've heard this one before." Trust me I get it, so have I! But this time it's different. I'm not the guru guy sitting from his throne trying to teach the little guy how to ride a bike, meanwhile, I'm getting chauffeured everywhere I go. I'm Jeremy Boykin, a middle-class citizen who has won a few major victories, yet is ultimately still in the battlefield fighting for his dreams. I'm not here to help you skip the process, I'm just here to help you speed it up! Remember, this book is called Microwave Dreams, not Who Wants to Be a

Millionaire. I've never had a million dollars, so I can't teach you something I don't know. But I have chased every dream that I've ever had. How many people do you know that can say that? I want to not only help you chase all of your dreams, but also help you do it in half the time.

This book is called MICROWAVE DREAMS because if we're honest we all want our dreams to come true quickly. Nobody seems to want their dreams oven cooked! And that's totally understandable. When you're hungry you don't feel like waiting to eat, you want it NOW! If you are hungry for answers to make your dreams come true today, this book has all the straight-to-the-point tools you need to fulfill your appetite, without ignoring the necessary core principles that we all need to navigate through our journey. In life, there are certain things that are unavoidable like hard work, sacrifice, and pain. We all have to experience these things at some point in our journey. I say this because my book is not some shortcut manual that allows you to snap your fingers to success. Instead, it's the coach you need, mixed with a whisper from God & a nice little pat on the back for the tough days. It doesn't matter if you are an adult who has chased a thousand dreams or if you are a teenager who doesn't have a clue what to do with their life. By the end of this book, you will feel inspired, challenged, and transformed. CHANGE is the ultimate goal in mind because there is nothing more powerful than a changed mind.

If you are reading this book, then you are ready for change. Attempting to grow or change can be a very painful process, but nevertheless, it's always worth it. You deserve the best life that God created you for. You deserve to know your role on this planet. You deserve to be happy. You deserve to know where to place your passions. You deserve to know what it takes to make your Microwave Dreams come true at a faster pace. I promise I won't hold back on this journey and I vow to give you everything I've learned from my best moments, and everything I've learned from my worst. Turn on the timer, it's time to heat it up!

J. REMY INSPIRES

DRIPPIN IN PURPOSE

I was 21 years old living in a dirty 4-bedroom apartment with three of my best friends. I spent every weeknight getting high as a kite and the weekends were reserved for the turn up which consisted of clubs, women, and a lot of weed and alcohol. I didn't have a job and I had recently been suspended from junior college because my GPA was lower than the temperatures in Antarctica. During this time, I began to work at a women's retail store and I absolutely hated it. I was making a little over minimum wage and dating a chick who I'm pretty sure hated me just as much as I hated her. I don't know if I painted that picture well enough for you, but let's just say I WAS BEYOND MISERABLE AND SO LOST THAT I COULDN'T FIGURE OUT IF I WAS GOING OR COMING.

I had no direction. I had no identity. Truthfully, anyone could've walked up to me and told me who I was and I would've believed them because I didn't have a single clue who or what I saw when looked in the mirror. I remember there was a verse by a music artist named Kid Cudi who suffered from depression and it said, "I AM HAPPY THAT'S JUST THE SADDEST LIE." I remember singing that part of the song with such passion because that was my life in a nutshell. I was always trying to "stay positive" but that was a lot easier to quote than to apply. I didn't know myself so I didn't know where I was going. My purposeless life took me to a dark place that I'll never forget. However, it also taught me a lesson that I'll always remember. <u>A life without purpose is a life without boundaries and we all need boundaries because without them we'll never find our purpose.</u>

There is a major purpose for your life, but figuring out what it is can be very tricky. Finding your purpose can be a lot like dating. You date people because you ultimately see the potential in them being the one. When it comes to finding your purpose, you should do things because you actually believe that it may be what you were created to do!! In the event that it doesn't work out, it's totally okay because there are plenty of fish in the sea. Just like dating, your purpose is certainly in the sea. You just have to keep swimming until you find it. Many times it takes doing a few things that you like or love before realizing what you were created for. And guess what, just like with dating, eventually you find the one and voila: you're married to your purpose.

Your purpose often times comes in steps and the funny thing is you don't even realize it as it's happening. As you focus on applying yourself to things that you're passionate about, the puzzle pieces gradually come together on their own. If you can find a problem in the world that drives you crazy, I wouldn't be shocked if your purpose was wrapped into finding the solution to that problem.

Your purpose is given to you to help others. <u>Selfishness is never connected to purpose.</u> Purpose always helps the world become a better place. If what you love is not adding true value to society then it's not your God-given purpose. It's just something that you're really obsessed with, a hobby if you will. Purpose also isn't based on how much money you can make or how well you can feed your family. It's a God-given passion for something. It's not based on a desire for success. It's based on your desire to use your God-given gifts to do something significant for the world. If you don't know your purpose, think you know it but you're not confident, or you just discovered that your financial status has nothing to do with your purpose, I would strongly suggest that you take some time to sit down and consider how you can make a real difference in this world with the gifts and abilities that you already have.

The hardest thing about finding my purpose was that I was so caught up in who I wanted to be more than who I KNEW I was created to be. Have you ever seen someone so cool with lots of money, nice cars and fancy clothes, and you tried to emulate them because you want what they have? That, my friend, will throw you all the way off from finding your purpose. As a matter of fact, be careful trying to chase success instead of significance because you may be chasing a path that leads to depression and not even realize it. You may be chasing a road to addiction and not even realize it. You may be chasing a journey of loneliness and not even realize it. We see people at the "top" doing so good (supposedly), but realistically they could be dying on the inside and constantly searching for more. The only true satisfaction that they have in comparison to others is the luxuries of being financially set. They usually aren't as happy as they seem because they didn't chase significance. A lot of times we assume just because a celebrity is rich and famous that they're living out their purpose, but the laws of purpose are not judged by a person's riches or glory, but by their honor, passion, and humility for what they do. In other words, if there is no honor in it, then it's not part of your purpose. If you're not passionate about it, then it's not part of your purpose. If there is no humility in it because you want the glory from it, then it's not your purpose.

Remember, selfishness is never connected to purpose.

SIGNIFICANCE > SUCCESS

A man may think everything he does is right, but God judges his motives. It's funny how most of us want to obtain the world's version of success. You know the money, cars, and clothes. Truthfully, success has become like eye candy. We just want it because it's superficially attractive. Fame is glamorous. Money brings lavish things and popularity means we'll never be alone again, right? Our motives for wanting to be successful are rarely from a place of selflessness. It's just all about us! Unfortunately, there aren't too many things people would find more important than success. If you haven't heard it already I'll be the first to let you know that there is something that blows being successful out of the water. It's called SIGNIFICANCE! A life full of significance is a life full of true purpose. You can be successful and not know your purpose, but when you're living a life full of significance, you're automatically dripping in purpose. I'm sure some of you may be thinking, "well what does a life of significance look like?"

It starts off with your motives being pure, your desire to make a change in the world, and your passion to help others in any way that you can. On the other hand, success is all about how you look or what you do and the scale of how well you're doing is solely based off of money or popularity. When it comes to chasing significance, you can be broke yet still living a life full of significance. You could literally be a nobody with 75 followers on Instagram and live a life full of significance. Significance adds value to the world. It leaves a legacy behind. Most importantly, it says a lot about your character. I can easily see how chasing significance may sound boring in comparison to chasing success, but if you really want to live in your purpose you have to value significance over success. <u>Success is more appealing to the eye, but it doesn't come with the same level of authenticity and longevity as significance. When you chase significance, you become popular for the RIGHT reasons.</u>

Just look at the lives of Martin Luther King Jr., Mother Teresa, or Gandhi if you think I'm lying. When you chase significance you inspire others to do the same. Chasing significance is so powerful that when you die your legacy lives through all the people you influenced. Again, success looks good, but significance is better. Success may make you happy at times but chasing significance will give you undeniable and unbreakable joy. The bottom line is this: if you chase success you may become a Kardashian, but if you chase significance you may have your own holiday. The choice is yours.

ONE PIECE AT A TIME

Have you ever heard someone say, "do you think he or she is the one for you?" in reference to marriage? I've heard this conversation a million times. Truthfully, I'm not sure if this concept is realistic or not, but hopefully one day I will get the chance to ask God. In the event that the concept of "the one" is realistic, I would like to assume that finding your purpose is a lot like finding "the one." As I stated before, many times it takes doing a few things that you like or love before realizing what you were created for! Yes, some people realize at an early age what they were created for and the difference they want to make in the world, but the majority of us reach our high school graduation with no clue of what's next. Or even worse, some of us reach our college graduation with no purpose, no job opportunities, and a whole bunch of college debt on the other side.

Ok back to finding "the one" ... YOUR PURPOSE AWAITS YOU, but you can't be afraid to rock the boat a little in order to figure out what your purpose is. If you feel as if you're passionate about something significant then attack it. If that thing doesn't work out, then find something else that's significant, that you're passionate about and attack it. Whatever you do, you have to trust part of one of the most popular scriptures which says, "all things work together for the good of those who love God." Romans 8:28. In other words, no matter how many times you try and fail or think you found your purpose and end up realizing it's not for you, I guarantee you every setback is a set up for a major comeback! God will use all of those moments, mistakes, and skills to show you how it all can be used for your ultimate purpose. It's a lot like putting a puzzle together: it can take a long time, you will think certain pieces don't fit, sometimes you will even lose pieces, but if you continue to try, eventually you will complete it and see the masterpiece. Let me share with you my puzzle piece story.

I played basketball my entire life. I was a standout student by my senior year of high school. However, due to problems at home and my spoiled mentality, I turned down three basketball scholarships. That landed me at a historically black college named, Alabama A&M without a single scholarship dollar to my name. I know. I was an idiot. My first day of college was a nightmare. I found myself in a new world without my girlfriend, best friends, or my star athlete identity. I was officially as lost as

I could ever be. After one year in Huntsville, Alabama, I moved to Auburn, Alabama where I had a ton of friends from high school. I spent approximately 4 years in this place trying to find myself by way of drugs, alcohol, and women. I thought I was cool, but really I was searching for identity in anything that came my way. Eventually, I started my first clothing brand called STL which stands for Sooner Than Later. This was how I found my first "piece" of purpose.

STL was a motivational clothing brand. I was determined to motivate the world through clothing with powerful quotes. Over the years, I went from just focusing on quotes to actually having a true passion for design. I designed many shirts and collections. I even opened up a store in Atlanta, Georgia for my clothing brand. Unfortunately, I lost my store, but soon after I began volunteering for a high school ministry with about 400 kids. Shortly after that, I started another clothing brand called, "God is the Plug." Then, it happened...

God spoke to me and told me that I will use my voice to change the world. I'm thinking, "ok cool, when does my rap career begin?" but He was specifically saying I would be an inspirational speaker. I was being called by God to use my voice to inspire people to change and help them heal.

I was hesitant at first because my dad was a preacher and I didn't want to be a preacher per se. However, I knew talking was my natural born gift because I love to talk more than most women (no offense). I also like people and I really love helping them grow and not make the same mistakes I've made. At the end of the day, it all made sense. Today, I'm not technically a pastor or minister, but I will speak, preach, talk, yell, or communicate a message of change anywhere at any time.

So, let's recap. The Sooner Than Later tee shirts with motivational quotes were the initial seeds planted. Then, I started volunteering at the high school ministry where I was able to give students the type of support and direction I never had when it came to making difficult decisions. Lastly, I started my second clothing brand, God Is The Plug, which started off just as tee shirts, but quickly turned into a movement (GOD IS THE PLUG parties) that consisted of music, merchandise, powerful messages and more. Those events granted me my first platform to speak consistently. From there, I was offered many more speaking opportunities at other locations. The point is, my purpose came in many pieces and in different seasons, but I was only able to find it by being consistent in trying to do something significant that I was also passionate about. If you only chase success, you'll never find your purpose. But if you chase significance then you'll not only find your purpose but you'll also be successful in your purpose.

WATER

Humans can't live without water. We absolutely need it to survive. Purpose is a lot like water. Not only because we need it, but also because it comes in various forms. For example, water can come in the form of ice, rain, sleet, snow, etc. Just like water, no matter what your purpose is, most of us are able to use it for different reasons. I mean seriously, water is so fascinating! It can erode land, grow plants, clean and hydrate our bodies, the list goes on. Many people put their purpose in a box, but I need you to know that ten out of ten times, most of us were put here for multiple reasons. Your purpose may be more than one thing or there may be more than one way to live out your purpose. Either way, just like H20, you will have multiple roles to play in this universal motion picture production called LIFE.

It's very important that you never let what you do define who you are. When I was in college, there was a guy named Gary at the Burger King and every time I went there would always greet me through the microphone with a loud, yet funny, "HELLO

TODAY!" Our entire interaction was always hilarious and full of intentional positivity. He should've been the poster boy for Kendrick Lamar's song, "Don't Kill My Vibe" because literally NO ONE could kill this man's vibe. Later, I heard from an associate of mine who worked at that same Burger King with Gary, that the management once told him he needed to calm down. Listen, this is such an important lesson. Some people let the job define them and others define the job! Gary's purpose was to inspire people to smile. His job was a cashier at Burger King. Just like water, Gary was multi-faceted. He could flip the burgers, take your order, count the money, and most importantly make you smile all at the same time. No matter what his job title was or how horrible of a job working fast food could be, Gary was still not defined by it and was clearly operating in his purpose! <u>Remember, your purpose is the difference you make NOT what you do!</u>

Below I have created a list of things you may do or want to do and the possible purpose(s) connected to it!

EXAMPLES:
Inspirational speaker – Inspire people to love themselves, to change, and to chase their dreams.
Make-up artist - Build people's self-esteem.

Barbers/Hairstylist – Build people's self-esteem and give them someone to talk to.

YouTube vlogger- Allow people to learn from your mistakes, give people someone to relate to, and provide people with an escape.

Music artist- provide people with an escape, give them advice, help them learn from your mistakes, all while giving them a reason to dance.

Doctor – Heal, save lives, provide hope

Lawyers - Defend, provide hope, properly tell a story

Police Officer - Serve & Protect

No matter where you are in life it's never too late to find your purpose. It doesn't matter if you are 13 or 65, purpose doesn't have an age limit. If you feel lost in life, just know that feeling lost is one of the many puzzle pieces that comes with finding your purpose. It happens, so don't quit at finding your purpose and don't you dare consider quitting on life! This crazy world needs you! Who knows who you are? You may have more purpose than anyone that's ever stepped foot on this planet. You may be the next Steve Jobs, Mother Teresa, Martin Luther King Jr., and Gandhi all combined into one. It may sound crazy now, but I bet none of them thought they would be as purposeful as they were from the beginning. Your purpose is unique, specially wrapped, and boxed just for you. <u>The world is always in need of</u>

additional change so remember when you run from or neglect your purpose, then you're neglecting the needs of the world. Always remember that.

START SOMEWHERE

Somewhere in America, there is someone who is considering starting up their own business, music career, or DIY YouTube page. Unfortunately, instead of just deciding to start it, they're going to think about it for weeks, months, or maybe even years. They'll never commit to fully starting because they are too afraid of the unknown. The spooky unknown, the one component so many are afraid of but none of us have ever met. We tend to fear something that isn't even promised to happen and we let it stop us from chasing our dreams. But, what if we flipped that sentence into a very bold declaration and instead say that we choose to be so brave that regardless of the unknown we won't let anything stop us from chasing our dreams! Way too often we have new light bulbs pop up in our heads and we throw those brand new light bulbs (aka new ideas) in the trash without even remotely trying to screw them in. What if we made a commitment to ourselves right now that from now on ALL LIGHT BULBS WILL BE RESPECTED! We know that our life could use some new light but the darkness has become so normal that a new light bulb would be too bright for us to handle. Well, I hate to burst your bubble but it's time to put your shades on and get up and scream, "I WANT THE LIGHT!" Your ideas could change the lives of so many people. Your ideas could shift this world in ways you would've never imagined. Your ideas could even fail and lead to you learning a lesson so valuable that you get to spend the rest of your life speaking to others on how not to make the same mistakes as you! There are so many possible outcomes that could come as a result of starting, but you'll never find out if you don't stop hiding from the light. Embrace the light.

PEN AND PAPER

In 2008 I drew my first sketch for my future clothing line called Sooner Than Later. It wasn't until 2009 that I actually released the first shirt. I literally sketched for an entire year before releasing my first product. I had an entire portfolio of sketches and ideas written down that I would pray to God would one day become a reality. And guess what, one day they did. I had people such as The Dream, Niykee Heaton, Young Joc,

Tyreese, and even Missy Elliot wear my brand. I'm not saying you need to wait a year to start moving your feet. As a matter of fact, please don't take that long. I just want to encourage you to get a pen and some paper and dream freely with every word and/or image as if they were going to jump off of the pages instantly. Not only will this give you a preview of your soon to be future but it will also give you something to get excited about. <u>Clarity is always found in a good plan</u>. So don't just sketch or write for fun, but consider this humble beginning as a vital step that will give you proper direction. It worked for me so I'm positive it will work for you!

COUNT THE COST

Have you ever been on social media and someone announces their new business and instead of getting excited for them all you think to yourself is "oh no not another one?" It seems like every day someone is starting something new—a new pyramid scheme, a new rap album, new blog, or someone just pursuing social media fame. Ultimately, I would never hate on anyone's dreams. However, the reason why I think most of us get tired of seeing people always start something new isn't that we hate their efforts, it's simply because most people who start up new business ventures end up quitting in less than a year. I just feel like if you didn't plan to finish it then why start it in the first place. But the reason why people quit or give up on their brand-new baby is simply because they forgot to do one major thing: COUNT THE COST. You have to be honest with yourself about how willing you are to stick to what you're desiring to start. If the idea in your head only seems worth your time when you dream of being rich, then it's not an idea worth pursuing. This is why before deciding to go into full pursuit we should have a serious conversation with ourselves about our ability to maintain and manage new projects. Helpful questions would be, do I have enough money, do I have the time, have I done the research, have I written a business plan, am I willing to persevere through the good and bad days. These are the type of questions you have to take the initiative to think through and answer or else you'll be just like your social media friends who started their business or brand that only lasted for all of 3 months.

Imagine if you were headed to the mall. Typically, before you start shopping you would count your money or check your bank account to see how much money you have. By knowing how much money you have it gives you the ability to wisely choose the purchases you decide to make. Counting the cost before starting something is a lot like counting money before shopping. It will save you from making purchases that don't come with a receipt.

The decisions we make can be costly ones if we aren't careful but when we choose to COUNT THE COST first, we save ourselves a whole lot of money, time, and embarrassment. Counting the cost can come with a lot of painful hard truth but I promise you it'll not only help you persevere through the stormy days but more importantly, it'll help you confirm that you're in the right race.

JUST DO IT

Once you've written a plan and counted the cost there's nothing left to do except—just do it! You will experience the most fear when you're prepared to start. There's something about being so close to starting your goal that makes you shy away from actually getting started. You begin to come up with excuses like I don't have enough money or I don't have the proper resources or nobody is going to support me. Let me tell you, all of these things are lies from the devil himself! You may not have enough money for YOUR long-term vision but you could still chase your microwave dream with the money you do have. <u>You can't just skip the humble beginnings and get straight to the fame & flash! Starting something without all of the desired resources builds character that you can't acquire on your own. And not having the proper tools to go after your dreams will also test your ability to adapt and be creative with what you already have.</u> NEVER LET

WHAT YOU DON'T HAVE OUTSHINE WHAT YOU DO HAVE.

I remember when I wanted to transition out of a company I was working at. I would literally stand and stare out of the windows that felt like prison bars constantly thinking about everything else I could be doing besides having to be there with the worst boss ever. Prior to working at this particular company, I had been passionate about inspirational speaking, but I had no experience whatsoever. I specifically remember hearing God tell me to "make videos" about 6 months before I started working at the company. But, I was convinced that it was all in my head and not actually God's voice talking to me. So months passed by and I continued to feel a strong desire to become an inspirational speaker. I didn't know where to start at first, but eventually, I started making videos. I didn't have a professional camera. I didn't have professional lights. My iPhone wasn't the newest version. I just had my old iPhone and a whole lot of passion with a desire to obey the suggestion giving to me by the voice in my head aka God's voice. In the process of making multiple inspirational videos, I began to feel so inspired that I decided to quit my job. Yes, I left my job without a backup plan, no interviews lined up, and not that much money in my bank account. It was a move I made merely off of faith. Shortly after quitting and about 7 videos later I received a message from a youth pastor who wanted me to come speak at their youth conference in Panama City and all expenses would be paid for. I was in complete shock. I could not believe that shortly after quitting my job I was receiving my very first speaking engagement! That, my friend, was the beginning to the rest of my life—inspiring the youth while getting the chance to travel all at the same time.

There's nothing like it & I'm so grateful he reached out. After the conference I reached out to the person who booked me to speak, wanting to know what made him pick me to be the main speaker. His answer—after seeing my Facebook video he knew he had to have me! This Facebook video he was referring to was a video I made with my old iPhone in my bedroom about how we have to stretch ourselves out of our comfort zone in order to pursue our destiny. I could've fainted because I realized I basically wasted an entire year ignoring God's voice, not knowing that he had something set up waiting on me the entire time.

This particular moment in my life taught me how you never know what's waiting on you which is why it's so important to always understand the essence of urgency and timeliness. When you think you're supposed to do something but you're slightly unsure, don't hesitate, just do it. Many times the very thing we are destined to do is attached to a bridge called fear that must be crossed somehow some way. Ultimately as humans, we mess up a lot so regret is basically a likely guarantee. On the flip side, there are all these ideas and dreams that you have that you have no excuse to ignore. If I was able to book my first speaking engagement off of a super raggedy Facebook video, then there's no telling what you can achieve if you just stop thinking about it and actually began to MOVE YOUR FEET.

One of the biggest keys to life that will give you an honest peace of mind is this: IT'S ALL ABOUT PROGRESS OVER PERFECTION. What I'm saying is as long as you're growing closer to your goal, destiny, or purpose then you're doing amazing for yourself. Don't get angry because things aren't how you imagined them to be. As long as you're making progress things are right where they're supposed to be. If someone can start up from scratch and get it perfected immediately, I guarantee they won't last because in order to have longevity with any dream, opportunity, or business you have to sweep before you mop. Sweeping represents the process of laying down the foundation for what's next. If you had a dirty floor at your house but you wanted it clean you would have to sweep it first because sweeping picks up the dust and miscellaneous things that are dirtying up the floor. Sweeping is like the foundation which allows us to appreciate the beauty of a nicely mopped floor. But if you have dirt, food, and trash on the ground and you start mopping without sweeping it may appear glossy, but it definitely will create a bigger mess without the foundation of it being swept. If we're honest with ourselves this is the concept that many of us try to chase our dream by. We don't want to walk before we run. We want to blow up instantly. We would prefer to skip the sacrificial stage of dream chasing aka sweeping. We literally want to heat the dream up in the microwave for 60 seconds and call it a wrap, but truthfully, we have no idea the mess that we're about to get ourselves into if we don't slow cook it. <u>Trying to skip the process when it comes to dream chasing is equivalent to taking some raw thawed out chicken and heating it up in the microwave and then just eating it.</u> Let me know how that works for you because I am pretty sure it could end up killing or seriously harming you. No matter your race, age, or religion there's a process to achieving your dreams. It is vital that you are willing to commit yourself to the process. Remember, just like the raw chicken, SHORTCUTS ALWAYS LEAD TO DEAD ENDS.

THE COMPARISON GAME

Did you know that there is only one you? Seriously, there isn't another person on this planet that can be you better than you can be you. No matter what they told you, you are truly a professional at being yourself. Whenever you have a dream that you want to chase always remember there may be ideas similar to yours, but there is only one you so those other ideas are not, and will never be the same as yours. When it comes to your dreams always make sure your main focus is the person in the mirror. You have to make a conscious decision daily to give your dreams 100% of your focus. <u>As soon as you start looking left and right you'll lose the tunnel vision and that'll be the same moment that you'll begin to lose control of your dreams.</u>

<u>Whenever we focus too much on other people's moves it can create lots of jealousy, insecurity, and doubt.</u>

I like to call this the COMPARISON GAME. There is so much danger in playing the comparison game. It will cause you to slow down because you'll spend so much time over-analyzing the moves of your opponents and peers that you'll gradually begin to abandon your original game plan. Whenever you're constantly critiquing yourself and forgetting that you have your own path, the comparison game can make you become really ungrateful. It will become super easy to not appreciate the blessings you already have. Let's be honest, <u>THERE IS A THIN LINE BETWEEN ADMIRATION AND THE COMPARISON GAME.</u> As a motivational speaker & designer, I admire many motivational speakers and owners of clothing brands. I watch some of the moves they make and I get so inspired and excited. But, if I'm not careful I can easily find myself transitioning from being inspired to comparing what they have to what I have. I begin to get thoughts like I'm not doing this good enough, I'll never be good as them, theirs is so much better, I should just quit now, etc. <u>The comparison game is literally self-sabotage at it's finest and it will stop you from being productive if you let it.</u> Truthfully, if I told you all of the crazy thoughts full of doubt and insecurity that I've had over the years you probably would be surprised that I even finished the very book that you're reading right now.

Unfortunately, if you're going to chase a dream you're probably going to accidentally end up playing the comparison game multiple times. For some reason, it's just human nature for us to constantly want a piece, if not all, of what someone else already has. But in order to achieve a dream as efficiently and quickly as possible, you have to stay in your lane. When it comes to dream chasing you can't continuously look left and right because that'll cause you to swerve. And swerving is how accidents happen. And when accidents happen dreams usually die. In other words, focusing too much on another person's race could cause you to give up on your own race. So always be thankful for what you have and remain focused on what's yours. Worrying about someone else's race could potentially put you in a mental race with someone who was never in the same race as you in the first place. You'll continuously stress yourself out competing against someone who doesn't even know you or heard of you or cares about what you have going on. Who would've ever thought we were so capable of creating our own distractions? Look forward and sometimes behind, but never left or right.

PRACTICE GRATITUDE

One of the main reasons we play the comparison game is because we don't appreciate what we already have. Sometimes we need to sit down and take a look back in the past and remember where we came from and recall all we've accomplished. If you haven't actually started working on your dream yet then this is still directed towards you because I'm sure you probably remember a time where you wouldn't have even taken the initiative to read a book like this. But now, look at you intentionally trying to grow! We must all be thankful for who we are today and what we have accomplished thus far. We must all practice gratitude. You may not be where you want to be and yeah you may feel discouraged because you feel as if you're running behind the originally planned schedule, but <u>comparing yourself to others instead of being thankful is so toxic that when you finally make it to the level that you've constantly compared yourself to, you won't even feel true satisfaction.</u>

Right now I bet you believe if you get what "THEY" (whoever you're constantly comparing yourself to) have you'll be satisfied but that's a lie. Stop lying to yourself. <u>IF YOU CAN'T APPRECIATE THE SMALL THINGS IN LIFE THEN YOU'LL NEVER BE ABLE TO PROPERLY APPRECIATE THE BIG THINGS EITHER.</u> If you can't learn to appreciate 10 sales then you'll never appreciate 100. If you can't learn to appreciate speaking engagements with 10 people then you'll never appreciate it when 1000 people show up. Instead of praying for what someone else has, learn to have gratitude for what you have already. More importantly, learn to celebrate other people's success and you'll find yourself living more blessed than before. When God sees that you are easy to please and you love to celebrate others He will bless you in ways that you could've never imagined. Jealousy is a disease and gratitude is the remedy. Don't let your lack of gratitude slow you down or hold you up. Wake up every day and say, "I'M SO GRATEFUL TO BE ALIVE. I'M SO APPRECIATIVE OF ALL OF MY MANY BLESSINGS—BIG AND SMALL. I THANK GOD FOR WHAT I HAVE & I WILL TAKE CARE OF IT AS BEST AS I CAN BECAUSE I REALIZE COMPARING MYSELF TO OTHERS WILL NOT SPEED UP MY PROCESS. I HAVE A FINISH LINE OF MY OWN THAT NO ONE CAN CROSS EXCEPT FOR ME."

SOCIAL MEDIA

Instagram, Facebook, Snapchat, and Twitter are four of the world's leading social media sites. I can't even lie, I love social media. It gives us all so much opportunity to know anything about everything and it also gives us a way to constantly be entertained. But as much as I love knowing what my friends are doing and getting a good laugh, what I love the most about social media is the ability to grow your business. I've heard so many older entrepreneurs talk about how lucky millennials are to be able to sell merchandise from their bedroom on their cell phones. And honestly, it really is a blessing. I have personably used Instagram and Facebook to make thousands of dollars with my clothing brands. Even as we speak right now I am consistently advertising my brand so shout out to all of the social media pioneers out there.

As much as I love social media there is one thing I absolutely hate about it: TOO MUCH SOCIAL MEDIA IS THE QUICKEST WAY TO FALL INTO THE COMPARISON GAME. When you get on social media you must be aware of the comparison game at all times. It's so easy to feel like you're constantly falling short of your goals when you see other people crushing theirs. Here's the truth: no matter how grateful you are for what you already have, if you're not careful, social media will kill your gratitude every single time. There were a couple of people that I admired that I experienced this with for years. I thought I was following these different brands and speakers because I was learning from them. But as I told you before there is a thin line between admiration and comparison. Somewhere along the way, I had lost my boundaries and the lines were crossed. I found myself angry on a weekly basis because my brand wasn't as big as theirs. I wasn't getting the same level of speaking opportunities as the other speaker. And we all know it's 10 times worse when we feel like what we have to offer is better than who we are comparing ourselves to.

It sucked so bad because during one particular season of my life I was so discouraged by my inability to "keep up" with the other speaker and brand. The other brand was way bigger than mine. But the dagger was people kept accidentally calling my brand the other brand's name that I was comparing my brand to! I said to myself I have to find a way to beat them, I have to be better than them. So, I watched them daily preparing to make moves that I hoped they wouldn't be able to keep up with. In my mind, the strategy that I was using with the opposing clothing brand was working so well that I started trying to use the same strategy with this inspirational speaker. I was watching him closely just like I was watching the other clothing brand. Between the clothing brand and the speaker, every move I made was being controlled by their moves. I was basically trying to be like them and outdo them but I wasn't focusing on my own personal finish line while doing so. This went on for about 6 months until one day God's voice smacked me in my face. These were His exact words:

"what I have for you is very different from what you're comparing yourself to. What they are doing is their choice but what I have for you is my will, and it's going to be massively effective and life-changing. Stop focusing so much on them and just focus on the task that I have given you."

Immediately after hearing those words, I ran to Instagram and unfollowed the clothing brand and the speaker who I was heavily influenced by. I didn't unfollow them out of hate or spite. I simply unfollowed them because I realized that if I continued to follow I might as well quit my dreams and go work for them. They were dictating all of my moves anyways.

So, let me ask you...who is it that you admire but sometimes you cross that thin line of comparison with? Maybe you need to focus more on the plan that God has given you or maybe you need to unfollow them on social media. No matter what you do, you must do whatever it takes to free yourself of the comparison game or else the odds of one day crossing your personal finish line will never be in your favor. Your dreams were given to you and only to you. It is your duty to always protect your dreams whether it's in person or on social media. When you are constantly comparing yourself to others it throws your mind off track and when your mind is off track your dreams are not being thoroughly protected. Protect your dreams at all cost or else when you die your dreams will rest in the graveyard with you.

THE X-FACTOR

Before you read this chapter, I want you to go find a private space. Tune everything out around you and forget everything you've ever been taught. I have a secret I want to share with you. Are you ready? Ok, take a deep breath...here it is: No matter how big your dreams are and no matter how fast you want them to happen, I have a secret weapon for you that will accelerate you into your destiny. It's called CHASING CRITICISM!!! Have you ever watched a video of a lion chasing its prey? It's pretty incredible to see how fast and ferocious a lion becomes once he sets his eyes on the prize! He doesn't give up until his mouth is full of flesh & blood & his stomach is screaming, "yummy." If you are serious about your dreams and you have your eyes on the prize then I need you to chase criticism the same way a lion chases its prey.

<u>Criticism will never feel as good as the results it can bring you.</u> When we think of criticism we automatically think of words like disrespectful, painful, or hurtful. No one wants to hear negative opinions about their idea or creation. But think about it like this, would you rather find out that your idea/creation is bad privately or would you prefer to release it without getting the proper feedback and be publicly humiliated? I can assure you that failing privately is a lot less painful than failing publicly. Trust me, I learned this the hard way. Chasing criticism allows us to fail privately while still having the opportunity to fix the failure. No one has to know that you missed the mark except you & the few people you allowed to give you constructive criticism. This, my friend, is the X FACTOR that can give you the edge that you've been looking for and push you towards your dreams with speed.

Chasing criticism will save you money & time—two things that you can't get back. Whether you've been vaguely brainstorming lately about a few ideas or maybe you have multiple vision boards at home, I TRIPPLE DOG DARE YOU to share the things you're on the verge of doing with a small group of people who can give you honest feedback. Maybe most of them will think your ideas suck or maybe they'll love them. You'll never know until you share it. <u>The cool thing about chasing criticism with the right people is sometimes new ideas are developed that would've never been thought of otherwise.</u> For example, there was a time where I was practicing for a speaking engagement with my friend and he told me he liked a certain part of my speech but hated the other half. By the end of practice, my entire speech was 10X better and sounded totally different. Thank God for my friend! I would've never realized how much work my speech really needed if it weren't for his criticism.

I know it's scary giving other people the right to tell you how they feel about your ideas or your work<u>. But the truth is, not only was Rome not built in one day but it also was not built by one person.</u> We are all very human. Therefore, we all need help in some capacity because we have preferences and blind spots which allows us to easily fail at a lot of things. Having a second, third, or fourth opinion will always put us in a better position to know what our chances are, and where we truly stand in whatever arena we're in. Never be a know it all. <u>Remember pride never produces positive results.</u> Be creative, but stay humble. Treat your dreams or your ideas like your very own little baby. Find you a small group of people you can trust with your baby. You may be thinking about writing your first book, you may have an idea for a non-profit organization, or maybe you make music. No matter who you are or what you desire to do, chasing criticism with the right people will make your microwave dreams come true a lot faster.

WHOSE CRITICISM CAN I TRUST?

The idea of chasing criticism isn't the most pleasant thought, right? You may even feel like I'm walking you right into an ambush. Honestly, if you chase criticism with the wrong people then you may be right. Remember, everyone doesn't deserve to have a say so about your dreams or ideas. There is such a thing as bad criticism and it usually comes at the most unwanted times. Nevertheless, chasing criticism can take you to higher places if you do it the right way with the right people.

<u>There is one thing that everyone who critiques you should have in common: they should all have your best interest in mind.</u> It doesn't matter if they are your family, friend, or co-worker. I repeat they MUST have your best interest in mind. Seeking criticism from someone that you can't trust to have your best interest in mind is always a bad idea. Find people who love you, appreciate you, respect you, or care about you. Also, find people who are very honest and not afraid to hurt your feelings. Here's

my personal break down on what your constructive criticism group (what I like to call, CCG) should look like:

- 50% of your CCG should consist of people similar to what I described up top: people who keep it real with you and love you, but they don't mind hurting your feelings. They also need to be knowledgeable of the arena that you are operating in. In other words, if you want to own a business make sure you ask someone who knows at least a little bit about entrepreneurship.

- 30% of your CCG should be people who typically disagree with everything you say or like. You know that person that you have a relationship with but they drive you crazy? Yes, yes, we all have at least one! Their honesty may be brutal but it could make you aware of your mistakes early on.

- The final 20% of your CCG may surprise you, but you need a couple of people who are a lot like you. Maybe you all share the same style or you like the same music. Whatever it is, it needs to be a group of people that share similar preferences as you.

This combination of people is not just a theory. This is the same ratio I used when developing my own personal CCG & those people and their critiques have greatly contributed to much of my success. Without them I would be a mess.

Just like anything else in life you have to find balance when it comes to your CCG. Everything they tell you will not be correct. Sometimes they will say things that are incorrect and hurt a lot. If you aren't capable of controlling your emotions than you shouldn't have a CCG. <u>The purpose of a CCG is to allow you to see your weaknesses and strengths before the world has the opportunity to tear you apart.</u> Either way, a CCG is there to help you not hurt you. Create your own and use them! Don't just ask for their critique and then ignore the information or advice given. Instead, humbly listen to everyone and find the common denominator critiques.

Every study I have ever done has shown me that every CCG has common denominator critiques. When this happens, you have officially struck gold! You get the opportunity of fixing whatever a majority of your CCG noticed. Having to go back and make adjustments to an idea or finished product isn't always fun. Personally, I hate it! Who wants to think they have a great idea or finished product only to find out that it's not so great or finished. That means more time is required, more energy and effort will be needed. It's all for the best though. Don't ever be discouraged by the criticism. Be patient enough to make the proper adjustments to your dreams that way you don't make a fool out of yourself publicly. Always know that you have the last word even over your

CCG. But if you choose your CCG the right way, I promise they will help guide you to the land of significance and success.

THE PROCESS SUCKS

Have you ever been going through something and someone told you to trust the process? You were really expecting them to give you some great non-cliché advice and they simply told you to trust the process. I don't know about you but that has happened to me more times than I can count. I just want to take a second and say THE PROCESS SUCKS AND IT HURTS LIKE CRAZY. As far as trusting the process goes, how can I trust something that I have never experienced before? I think we can all agree that it's pretty hard to trust something that we know very little about, and trust is typically earned not given. Some people would argue that since you've seen "the process" work for other people, you should trust that if it worked for them it will work for you. Although there is some truth to that statement, there is ZERO GUARANTEE that it will work for you. The bottom line is that when it comes to chasing our dreams, risking it all, and putting everything on the line, we would love to know that success awaits us on the other side. If "THE PROCESS" wants our trust then uncertainty, disappointment, and failure cannot be part of the package. Why? Because we feel entitled to our dreams coming true right now! Not tomorrow, not after the process, but RIGHT NOW!

<u>If this is how you feel, then you, my friend, are unfortunately struggling with an issue of entitlement! You want the gold without the grind. You want the purpose without the pain. You want the win without the work.</u> In sports, you can't win a championship without first playing a game and you can't play in a game without first going to practice. You can't even practice without first going to tryouts. <u>The funny thing is, everyone—from the people who you know to people who you don't know—will congratulate you after you win a championship, yet nobody will tell you congratulations for going to tryouts. Society will always glorify and highlight our accomplishments over our efforts. But, I just want to let you know that your efforts matter! As a matter of fact, your efforts are necessary and your process begins as soon as you sign up for tryouts!</u> Many times, starting is the hardest part because you feel so far away from your championship game. In other words, the PROCESS CAN SEEM VERY INTIMIDATING, so we shy away from it. The good news is the process can be sped

up, but the bad news is you can't skip it. <u>Truthfully, the desire to skip the process is something that I think we all share, but the reality of it is that people hit the lottery and win millions every day, yet a majority of them don't die as millionaires. What I'm saying is that no matter what your goal is, you don't need to obtain it if you can't sustain it.</u> The process will give you the tools you need to not only win the championship but to remain a champion. IT'S NOT JUST ABOUT GETTING THERE, BUT RATHER KNOWING HOW TO STAY THERE!

Have you ever tasted a piece of cake so good that you wanted to slap somebody's mama? I have! My grandma used to make this cake that was so delicious and I would eat several slices as if catching diabetes wasn't a real thing. It was a gigantic TRIPLE LAYER YELLOW CAKE. It was moist, and every layer had a ridiculous amount of icing on it which made it ten times better than your average cake. The only unfortunate part about this cake was that it took ten years to make. YES, TEN FREAKIN' YEARS. Okay, okay, maybe it was just one day, but it felt like ten years! My grandma would slave over this one cake all day long. I would run in and out of the kitchen eating the batter out of the bowl, asking her if it was ready yet because I was so anxious to eat the cake. But, despite how impatient I was, my grandma understood that the cake had a certain process and had to be cooked properly in order to turn out the right way. But I didn't care about the process AT ALL...I just wanted the final product.

I don't know what your dream is or how hard your process will be, but I can guarantee you that there is a lot of purpose in your process. Don't try to skip the process. <u>If you aren't willing to persevere through the process, then you don't deserve the final product.</u> Success is earned not given and dreams don't come true overnight. The energy you're spending complaining and comparing could be energy well spent on grinding towards your dreams. Do yourself a favor and say "I DO" to the process. Yes, I'm asking you to put a ring on the process. If you love the idea of living in your purpose and being successful, then I suggest that you make a commitment to the process today! Look the process right in the eyes and say, "I don't know where you will take me or how long it will be, but I'm committed till death do us part!" When we develop a mentality where we just want to grind, be impactful, and be consistent more than we want the final product, the truth is success will fall in our lap. LITERALLY! There's no time to play the comparison game or focus on our shortcomings.

The bottom line is once you say I DO to the process, DIVORCE is off the table and the real work begins. Just like getting married to a person, being married to the process is going to be difficult. Some days you will ask yourself why did I commit to this. In those moments, you have to remind yourself that you can't quit when you're one step closer to where you want to be. If a deal goes bad you learned a lesson. If your new business failed, you learned a lesson. If your new social media plan failed, you learned a lesson. If you lose friends or family throughout your process YOU LEARNED A LESSON. No matter what angle you look at it from, there are never LOSSES but only LESSONS. The process won't be easy, but I promise if you have a dream it's necessary.

THE CHEAT CODE

Honestly, there's not much anyone can say to make going through the process popular. The process isn't glamorous and it involves a lot of pain; therefore, it'll never go viral or become trendy. But what if I told you I have the cheat code to the process? What if I told you there were several major tips I could give you to help you speed up the process? Each tip could change your life, but the question is if you knew it would you apply it? Let's find out!

1. STAY FAITHFUL TO YOUR FEW - I started volunteering for a high school ministry over three years ago not knowing that one day I would become a youth motivational speaker. I

didn't start volunteering in hopes of becoming a speaker, but instead, I started because I wanted to help kids not make the same life mistakes as I did. I was one of many volunteers, so I didn't feel special or important. I didn't have any opportunities to get on stage and speak the way I wanted. At one point, I didn't even feel appreciated. However, I had a small group of kids that I was supposed to check on and call/text on a weekly basis. I was committed to that. I had my ups and downs initially, but I ultimately went from a decent volunteer leader to a well-known and highly respected leader. I still serve in that ministry today and I love those kids with all of my heart. It took time, but it was like the more I was willing to be faithful to what I currently had, the more responsibility and opportunities came knocking at my door. Maybe you currently have responsibilities or opportunities in your possession and you're not taking good care of what you have yet you're desiring more. Let me tell you this, MORE WILL NOT COME UNTIL YOU PROPERLY VALUE WHAT YOU ALREADY HAVE. If you want to speed up the process, take better care of your current position, business, or opportunity. And if you have none of the above, then work on improving yourself, whether it's your attitude or your character. No matter how you look at it, you can't have more until you improve the way you treat having less.

2. STAY FOCUSED ON YOUR DESTINATION - Distractions come in so many forms. The one that seems to do the most damage these days is the media. Whether it's the news, tv, or social media, it's so easy to feel like you are so far behind in life. Seeing other people's success should be used as motivation, but most of us become discouraged by the simple thought of "I'm not there yet." If you and a friend were traveling somewhere you've never been before, you would type in that one destination on your GPS and stay the course. You wouldn't pick up your friend's phone and type in a different destination or take your eyes off the road. You would stay focused on the one destination that you originally typed into your GPS because focusing on anything else would be pointless and dangerous. No matter what's happening around you, the more you stay focused, the further you will go. Distractions will always be a factor because in order to be great, we have no choice but to fight and constantly push through the unknown. Many times, people, the lies in your head, and insecurities will try to blind you, but remember nothing can stop someone who knows where they're going. LOCK IN!

3. DON'T QUIT - This is probably the most cliché advice ever, right? But the reason why it's such a repetitive piece of advice is that it's the bottom line of all bottom lines. If you commit to something and never quit it, you allow yourself to become better developed and wiser than most. Time is the greatest teacher. If you stay committed to a job, dream, or goal long enough, promotion is bound to happen. Unfortunately, because we are such microwave dreamers, we expect everything to happen overnight. We often miss out on the unknown benefits of sticking around through the storm. Listen, I have quit almost every job that I've ever had simply because I knew I wasn't built to work for other people. But I have never quit on my dreams of owning a million-dollar clothing line, becoming a world renown speaker or writing a New York Times bestseller. You need to learn the difference between quitting and over-committing. I should've never committed to those jobs in the past because I wasn't serious about working at those places. But, I've always taken my dreams as serious as a heart attack. If you really want to speed up the process, make sure you only commit to things you are 100% serious about and NEVER QUIT. Not quitting won't be easy, but if

you can't ride out the storms of staying committed, then you'll never reach your destiny.

At the end of the day, we are always saying we want someone else's lives. We want to be like the next superstar athlete, the next movie star, or the next social media famous person. In order for us to truly aspire to be more wealthy, confident, or talented, like the stars, we have to be willing to go through a process just as hard as theirs. It's very easy to want what someone else has, but it's much harder to endure the process they went through to get what they have. I once heard a famous speaker who lost his arm from a football injury say, "so many guys want to be a big-time speaker like me, but do you want to lose your professional football career like me? Do you want to go through tons of surgeries like me? Do you want to only have one functioning arm like me?" As a fellow speaker, I think so highly of this guy but I'd be lying if I said I want his process because I don't. I can't imagine all the pain he has endured to get where he is today. We must quit chasing other people's popularity without properly understanding their process. There's a customized process that we must all go through to get whatever the big man upstairs has for us. I guarantee you that parts of it will suck but it will all be worth it in the end. Trusting the process would be ideal but not always a reasonable request. So, when your tank is on E and you feel like quitting, I challenge you to STAY COMMITTED TO THE PROCESS. Remember, success will only treat you as good as you are willing to treat the process. YOUR PROCESS WON'T BE PERFECT, BUT LONG AS YOU STAY COMMITTED, IT WILL BE PROGRESSIVE! YOU GOT THIS!

BUILD YOUR OWN BOAT

THIS WORLD OWES YOU NOTHING. I REPEAT: THIS WORLD OWES YOU NOTHING. IF ANYTHING, YOU OWE THE WORLD. YES! YOU OWE THE WORLD. I assume since you're reading this you have breath in your lungs and a brain that thinks. Therefore, you have no excuses to not find a way to leave your mark on this planet by achieving your dreams before your life is over. But the thing is, every single choice you make and every single thought you think will determine how much you accomplish. Let me let you in on a little secret, DREAMS ARE EXPENSIVE...VERY, VERY EXPENSIVE. Making your dreams come true may cost you everything: time, energy, money, relationships, social life, or even your belongings. Literally, whatever you have is up for sacrifice when it comes to making your dreams come true. I know this isn't the most encouraging chapter but I want to set you up for success by keeping it real with you upfront.

I remember years ago I got booked for a speaking engagement and the week before I was just scrambling for change out of my piggy bank to eat. I was turning down opportunities to take well-paying jobs just to focus on my own business knowing that my bank account was on the verge of going in the negative. YOUR DREAMS WILL NOT BE FREE. You will have to pay for them in sweat, sacrifice, and hard work! It doesn't matter what color you are, your dreams aren't free. It doesn't matter if you work a 9-5 or not, your dreams aren't free. It doesn't matter if you're really talented, your dreams will still cost. It doesn't matter if you feel like God told you to do it, your dreams still will not be free! The only thing that makes the dream come true is work, work, work, and more work. The more you grind, fail, and adjust, the further you will go. But first, you must accept the fact that dream chasing is a journey that feels like torture at times. The disappointment and the failure will make you want to pull your hair out and give up. I've even experienced deep moments of depression and sadness while chasing my dreams.

But the sooner you learn to expect failure, the faster you'll learn how to work through it.

FALSE EXPECTATIONS

We live in a world full of imperfect humans including yourself. Things will go wrong and not happen as planned more often than not. Sometimes it will be your fault and sometimes the fault will belong to others. But it's not what happens to us that defines us, it's how we respond to uncomfortable circumstances that determines the person we will become. In this game called life you will get hit, stomped on, and beat down, but the question is, will you get back up and how hard will you hit back once you're back on your feet? It's a lot easier to take a blow when you expect it than when you don't expect it. Imagine if you were hanging out with someone very attractive of the opposite sex and while you're staring deep into their eyes, Mike Tyson the famous boxer known for knocking people out, came out of nowhere and punched you right in the mouth. It's a good possibility that his blow to your face may kill you because he caught you off guard. Not to mention, he is a former world champion who once had a licensed fist. On the other hand, imagine if Mike took a swing at you while you were focused and expecting his blow. It would still extremely hurt, but you would have a better chance at living through the pain because you were expecting it.

Just like unexpected pain, FALSE EXPECTATIONS will kill you. It will kill your drive. It will kill your motivation and most importantly it will kill your spirit. When you have a certain expectation in mind and it doesn't go your way, it can throw off the entire game plan in ways that will set you back days, weeks, months, or maybe even years. But if you live a life constantly aware that your perfect plan could fail at any time, then you, my friend, are setting yourself up for many lessons that will one day turn into success. Believing in yourself is a must. However, I encourage you to always chase your dreams knowing that any day something could go terribly wrong. I'm not suggesting that you live in fear, but I am suggesting that you live in reality and with a high level of awareness. Every year multiple athletes have career ending injuries that they didn't expect. A majority of small businesses fail yearly day in and day out. People end up homeless who were once wealthier than you are right now. BAD THINGS HAPPEN TO GOOD PEOPLE every day. Therefore, you are not excluded from the possibility of bad things happening to you. But, you are able to control how ready you are for those moments from an emotional standpoint. Live your life being very grateful for whatever blessings you already have. And whenever things go south of what you expected, look for the lesson in the experience. Spend less time expecting things to always go your way and more time learning lessons from every failure or let down. <u>No matter what the circumstance is there is always an opportunity to grow from it, you just have to search for it.</u>

OWNERSHIP

The easiest way to figure out the lesson in a situation is to walk over to a mirror and say "what could you have done better?" Don't worry, the mirror won't talk back but hopefully, your conscience will. <u>In every circumstance, there is always an opportunity to not only learn a lesson but to take ownership.</u> Ownership is something that is super taboo and rare in today's society. EVERYONE HATES TO BE WRONG AND PRIDE BASICALLY RUNS OUR LIVES. <u>If you can figure out a way to be so humble that you constantly search for a way to see what you could've improved, you will outrun every microwave dreamer around you!</u> I know the crybaby inside of you is screaming, "but it's never my fault!!" Tell him/her to shut up! It's always something you could've improved. Maybe you could have communicated better, put forth more effort, created a better plan—no matter what you're trying to do with your life there's always room for growth.

I remember one day my friend, Ying, who prints my t-shirts for my clothing brand GOD IS THE PLUG forgot to call me before 4 p.m. . Earlier that day she told me she would let me know when my shirts were ready for pick up before that time. I really needed those shirts that day and I didn't get them because when I decided to call her at 3:30 p.m., she said she was headed home soon. I asked why didn't she call me and she said she thought I would've assumed the shirts were ready already because it was so close to 4 p.m.. I was so angry but then I stopped and evaluated the situation only to realize that I had to blame myself. Here's how I see that situation: if I would've woke up earlier that day I would've completed all of my busy work sooner, which would've given me more time to check on my shirts being done. If I would've contacted her sooner I would've had more breathing room to make time to pick up the shirts. Ultimately, I realized I had the opportunity to take full ownership and I immediately apologized to Ying.

Furthermore, that situation taught me that I can't wait for someone else to do what I should be doing. It's my brand so I can't expect anyone to put my brand first like me. <u>Blaming others will never help you build your dream. It will, however, cost you a lot of time and cause you to never learn the lessons needed that would've eventually propelled you into your destiny.</u> So no matter if it's your annoying boss, annoying coworker, or your annoying employee, always look for a way to take ownership. It's attractive, helpful, and needed. <u>Taking ownership won't always be easy but it will bring you closer to your dreams at a faster pace.</u> Stop finding ways to blame other people and accept the fact that your dreams are on your shoulders...THE BURDENS ARE ALWAYS YOURS TO CARRY.

GO GET IT

May I ask you a question? When someone cooks you a delicious hot meal what do you do? When you're thirsty and you have a cold beverage in the fridge what do you do? The answer is YOU GO GET IT! You don't hesitate. You don't contemplate. You just get up and GO GET IT!!! When it comes to your dreams you must be the same way: JUST GO GET IT. <u>Stop waiting for permission.</u> It's time to execute that innovative idea that you've been putting off. That thing you wrote down in your journal that you don't have money for...it's time to take baby steps towards it. <u>When God sees you moving towards your dreams I guarantee you He'll give you the resources you need when the time is right. But you have to stop waiting for permission.</u> No one ever said, "Hey Jeremy you should start a clothing line, or become a speaker, or write a book!!" I just knew the desires of my heart and I acted on them. I didn't know if my ideas would work or fail, but I did it anyway! Why? Because I believed in myself. So, I have to ask what is it that you want to do that you're quietly waiting for someone to give you permission to do? And furthermore, why are you waiting for permission? Maybe you struggle with feeling insecure in your ideas, maybe you're afraid to fail, or maybe you're just lazy. Either way, your dreams aren't going to come true without you putting in the work. So, I need you to get up and GO GET IT!!

ISLAND

At this point, I hope you feel motivated to grab your dream by the horns. But if for some reason you don't, I have to ask you these questions: do you believe your dreams are just going to come to you? Do you believe that your dreams are going to build themselves? Do you believe somebody is going to come save you? I want you to imagine yourself on an island all alone. An island that you are not happy to be on. There's no one but you, wild, dangerous animals, a ton of natural resources and you have to figure out a way to get off this island ASAP! Nobody is coming to save you and there isn't a magic boat being sent your way. Your only way off is to build your own boat and paddle your way back to society. No one can build it for you except for you. How the rest of your life pans out is completely in your hands and up to you. Just imagine all the promises you made yourself, all the things you wanted to achieve, all the places you wanted to go. Oh, and what about your loved ones. If you don't get off this island you'll never be able to keep your word to your significant other, your parent(s), or even your kids. Everything is literally riding on if you can build your own boat!!!

This is a lot like how chasing your dreams look. Everything is riding on you. No one can do the work for you but many will be affected by your choice to not do the work. If you don't chase your dreams not only will you not live your best life but you will hinder those around you from benefiting from your best life. You may be saying I want to build a boat but I just don't know how. Or maybe you've been trying to get off the island for a long time and you're extremely tired. I don't know if you're supposed to be a future author, music artist, movie star, designer, hair stylist, business owner, or things I didn't even name. All I know is you have to build your boat one step at a time and never give up until you're off that dangerous island full of laziness, fear, and insecurities. YOU HAVE TO GO GET IT. Rome wasn't built overnight and your boat won't be either. You will get tired of searching for resources and building, but I would rather die trying than die knowing I gave up. Just like the boat, your dreams are capable of being built. I just need you to get up and make it happen, captain. Remember, nobody is coming to save you because if they were, they would already be there. But don't panic because you, my friend, are not only a professional boat builder but you are a real dream chaser as well. Let's go baby, it's either sink or swim or in this case BUILD OR DIE.

SQUAD

S QUUAAADDDDDD!!! My brother Erskine loves to scream that word at the top of his lungs no matter where we are. I'll never forget this time we were taking a picture with a famous speaker and he just randomly screamed "Squadddddddddd!!!" during the photo session. Sometimes I wish he'd chill-out with the yelling, but honestly, I respect the fact that he's so proud of his squad. I'm also glad that I can say I'm part of that squad due to our very strong brotherhood. Just in case you don't know, a squad is essentially a small group of people who share a common identity or maybe a common goal. Basically, your squad is your friends; not your associates or coworkers, but your true friends. They are the people who we spend tons of our time around, that not only shape how we see ourselves, but also how we see the world.

Your SQUAD can play a major role in who you will become. Your SQUAD can either push you forward or hold you back. If you show me your squad, I can show you your future. No, I'm not a psychic but I do know that roses don't grow out of concrete. In other words, in order to properly flourish in life, we need to have the right foundation. Good friends are like good soil; they help you properly grow. Bad friends are like cheap soil, they slow down your growth. Maybe you have a friend that doesn't necessarily hold you back, but they don't necessarily push you forward. Let me tell you something, we only get one life & time is not on our side. Anyone that's a part of your squad better be helping you grow spiritually, mentally, financially, emotionally, or physically. If they aren't bringing anything to the table then you can't afford to have them in your squad. Remember, I said good friends are like good soil; that means you must be able to build with them. You grow together. You reach goals together. You change for the better together. There's nothing worse than having a friend that you keep constantly having to look back at wishing they would do more or try harder. It's draining and sometimes heartbreaking to try to carry dead weight along your journey. That is why it's so important to choose your squad wisely, because your squad always plays a major role in helping you accomplish your dreams.

I understand this probably came off a little harsh, but this book is called microwave dreams, not crockpot dreams. I'm trying to help you get to where you want to go in a timely fashion, & honestly, an inadequate squad is the one component that could ruin everything you've learned in the other eight chapters or even life. You are who you hang around, and if that statement bothers you then you probably need a new squad ASAP. You need a great squad. A great squad has great energy. Squad energy should be positive, supportive, and most of all authentic. When you have the right squad, your dreams are in safe hands. Unfortunately, in today's society, dysfunctional relationships and friendships are pretty much the norm. Just in case you're unfamiliar with what a great squad should look like, I'll give you a little more insight on who you don't need in your squad:

- Negative Nancy- Someone with negative energy who make it very difficult for positive energy to flow on a continuous basis.
- Dream Killer- The person who you have to suppress your dreams & ideas for
- Hater- Someone who always see a problem with everything you have, do or create.

- Leech- Someone who only comes around when it benefits them. They take, take, take, and then take some more. Rarely give.
- Sloth- The person who always talks about what they are going to do but is too lazy to execute.
- Guilt Tripper - the person that makes you feel bad for your success because they aren't successful in the same capacity.

Sheesh. I'm sure by now you have at least one friend that comes to mind for some of those categories. I want to be clear about this. Some people are in our lives for us to invest in them, but even investments only last for so long. <u>Before you invest in anyone you need to first invest in yourself.</u> Because anyone that fits into any of those 6 categories is a person who probably lacks self-awareness. If they aren't aware, they aren't intentional. If they aren't intentional, there is no way the two of you can be moving toward a common goal.

Make sure your Squad consists of genuine people. People who want to see you succeed but love you enough to call you out on your crap. You need people in your corner who want to invest in you the same way you invest in them. Never compromise your dream for people who are leeching off your vision. Instead, surround yourself with people who you can trust your vision with. You need a dependable squad, and a dependable squad requires trustworthiness. When you have the right squad, your dreams are in safe hands. <u>The environment in which we spend our time in and who we spend our time around will always determine how much fruit our time produces.</u> If you want to go far quickly, get you a solid squad. Remember, teamwork makes the dream work.

GET READY

So many times we pray and cry about getting our way in certain areas of our lives, but truthfully, if we were to get what we wanted, we wouldn't know what to do with it. The money would give us too much opportunity to make dumb decisions. The relationship would make us lose focus on our goals. The business would fail so hard that we would lose everything we own. <u>The best way to prosper in life is to figure out what God's plan for you is, and then prepare for it as if it were all unfolding before you tomorrow! When we prepare for what we are praying for, we show God that we are serious about what we're asking for. When we show God that He can trust us with his heart's desires then it makes it so much easier for Him to bless us.</u> However, more often than not, we think we're ready for His blessings way too soon.

Truthfully, as humans, we can be so dumb. We do so many stupid things that I can't imagine how often God laughs at us. Just think for a second about that toy you begged your parents for when you were five that you stop playing with after one week. Think about that new car you crashed a week after getting it that you cried for....or maybe that's just my story LOL. Think about that good-looking girl or guy you dated that you pushed away. Maybe think about that money you received that you can't even remember how it was spent. Over and over again we pray & ask for things that we are absolutely not ready for. We believe that we are deserving of everything we want in life just because we desire it, but it's foolish for us to think that way. <u>With any great reward comes great responsibility and if you aren't ready to take your responsibility to the next level, stop expecting next level blessings.</u> Let me say it this way: **if you want more than you already have, then figure out how to have more discipline than you already have.** <u>Crying for more without preparing for more makes it obvious that you don't even realize what you're asking for.</u> Remember, God loves you so much that He's not going to give you anything that's going to cause you to self-destruct. Jeremiah 29:11 says that God knows the plan that He has for you. I challenge you to figure out God's plans for your life (purpose) and then begin preparing for it asap.

For example, if you want to be a pro athlete, start taking care of your body like a pro athlete. If you want to be a music artist, start practicing for future performances now before you ever have your first tour date. If you want to be social media famous or a YouTuber, then you need to start posting quality pictures and videos NOW as if you had already gone viral. If you want to be a millionaire, why aren't you reading tons of books on how to manage your money? Listen to me, <u>no diamond ever goes undiscovered—it only becomes shinier during the waiting process.</u> In other words, **you must get ready for what you desire with full confidence knowing that your time will come and when it does you need to be ready.**

Just in case you don't understand what I'm saying take James Harden as an example. James Harden is a six-time Allstar NBA basketball player who plays for the Houston Rockets and currently leads the NBA in scoring. As if killing it on the court wasn't enough, he also has a $200-million-dollar contract with Adidas. He seriously needs to let me borrow some money. Before James-the-Beard-Harden became the superstar that the world knows him to be, he was a low-key superstar. He was coming off of the bench as the 6th man on The Oklahoma City Thunder basketball team along with the famous Russell Westbrook and Kevin Durant who have both won MVP awards over the past few years. Alright, let me put this into perspective for all of you who don't watch basketball or have any understanding of what I just said. Russell, Kevin, and James were all on the same team. They and the team were really good. Although only two of them started (Russell and Kevin) the team was always known for all three stars. Watching them was so amazing as Russell and Kevin were the top two leading scorers on the team, and Harden was the third leading scorer. Since they didn't have a great second-string lineup, the coach thought it would be best to bring Harden off of the bench even though everyone knew he was just as good as the two superstars playing in front of him. As a former basketball player, I have seen firsthand how discouraging coming off of the bench can be. Especially when you know you're just as good or better than the player(s) who are getting all the shine, waiting for your big opportunity can cause you to gradually lose confidence in your talent. Trust me, every year athletes all across the world sit on the bench as their skillset collects dust. Harden was the exception because he was intentional about capitalizing on every single bit of playing time he received. He had a MVP mentality even though he wasn't a starter. He also had a very popular reputation for his hard work ethic in practice.

In 2012, Harden won the 6th man of the year award and coincidently that same year his contract with Oklahoma also concluded. James's hard work led to the Houston Rockets offering him a five-year contract for $80 million. This was huge because the three amigos (Harden, Westbrook, and Durant) were so close to building a basketball dynasty. But when Oklahoma had their chance to keep James, they only offered him $54 million. And, let's be honest, they kind of made Harden's choice too easy. You don't have to be a math scholar to realize that 80 is a big difference from 54 on any scale. Obviously, Harden decided to go to Houston. Looking from the outside in, Harden's decision was one of the best ones he's ever made in his life. In his last season with Oklahoma, he averaged 16.8 points per game and in his first season with Houston, he averaged 25.9 points. As of February 4, 2019, James Harden is the leading scorer in the NBA averaging a whopping 36.3 points per game. Oh, and did I mention in 2017 Harden received a $228-million-dollar contract extension that broke NBA payday records!?!

Harden is winning in life & clearly was more than prepared for what he prayed for. He did his best under the circumstances he was in. He couldn't shine 100% with his first team because he was coming off of the bench but he didn't let that stop him from growing into a better player. He didn't complain or act as if the world owed him anything, he just kept growing and getting better. He trusted his work ethic and his preparation knowing that it would all pay off one day. He was even best friends with the two guys who he knew he was just as good as, even though they were starting in front of him every night. There's a lesson here for all you haters and frenemies. Instead of being a certified hater, support those people who are where you want to be, continue to prepare for what you desire, and always trust that your time is coming. There's never a reason to be jealous because if it were your time you would already be there. I'm sure there are many more, but Harden's story is the perfect example of how big the blessings can be when you prepare for the opportunity. I don't know too many sixth men that would be prepared to transition from coming off the bench to becoming the face of an NBA franchise. Harden was prepared. The question is: will YOU be prepared to transition from your current season to your new one when opportunity calls your number? Will YOU be able to capitalize on the opportunity of a lifetime when it comes knocking on your door? Seriously, be honest with yourself right now and answer these two questions:

1. What are you praying or hoping for?

2. Are you preparing your hardest for it?

I don't know your hopes or prayers, but if your answer to #2 is yes, then I hope you're not fooling yourself with false preparation. I hope you are preparing with every possibility in mind because as awesome as it is to be prepared for opportunity, not being prepared sucks.

When I was 20, I prayed for my former clothing brand, Sooner Than Later Clothing, to be in a retail store. Well, fast forward nine years later, I received a HUGE check from a retail store that bought a TON of shirts from my other brand, God is the Plug. They put my GOD IS THE PLUG brand in over 60 of their stores across 13 states. This was the biggest thing that ever happened to me. I was so happy! But, it was a huge learning experience. During this process, I learned a lot about everything I was not prepared for and it wasn't fun at all. There was certain lingo that I didn't understand very well when it was time to discuss the terms of the agreement. There were all types of details that I didn't think to address that the retail company's buyer had to bring to my attention. The worst part of it all was that I didn't have any of my legal documents yet. GOD IS THE PLUG wasn't officially a registered business nor did I have it trademarked. So, you mean to tell me that you had your GOD IS THE PLUG brand in over 60 stores and 13 states with no trademark Jeremy? YES, I KNOW. I'M AN IDIOT. [Hey, don't think too fast. It's already taken care of now you little thief LOL. I know what you were thinking and it's too late for you to grab it].

To be honest, I took a big risk by putting my brand in stores while knowing that it wasn't legally covered. But because an opportunity came knocking, I answered the door in my pajamas totally not ready. I hadn't taken a shower, I wasn't fully dressed, and I had barely brushed my teeth (metaphorically speaking that is). I went on a date with opportunity unprepared and almost missed my date with destiny. The worst part of this movie scene has yet to be told. When the BIG CHECK was finally sent to me in the mail after a 30-day wait, it was paid to the order of God is the Plug. And guess what? My birth name is Jeremy Boykin, not God is the Plug. I had no legal proof that God is the Plug was my business, so I couldn't cash the check. Just know the process I had to go through in order to get the check cashed required a 4 hour drive. SMH. This was by far one of the most frustrating moments I've ever experienced. I remember being so angry because I really needed that money for my next business endeavor. I couldn't believe I had a check for thousands and thousands of dollars that I couldn't cash. This circumstance forced me to cover my legal tracks swiftly and carefully. Not only because I had to cash my check, but also because I didn't want the next situation to be me receiving a letter telling me that I didn't own my brand because someone had stolen it.

I need you to learn from my story. Don't wait until your dream comes true to prepare, because if opportunity knocks at the right wrong time you won't know whether to smile or frown. Embarrassment will become a real possibility and another opportunity like that may never come again. Stay ready so you don't have to get ready. <u>Readiness attracts steadiness. If you stay ready, then you will always be in a position to attract continuous blessings.</u> I'm sorry but there is no cheat code for this one guys. You have to work hard in order to get what you want in life. And you have to work even harder to keep it! But every second is worth it because hard work builds character and character is what sustains success. So, all in all, I leave you with this: if you want a particular relationship, or a certain amount of money, or even some sort of business or career, start preparing for it now. Work so hard to become the person that is truly prepared to the point that God has no choice but to say "you deserve it." Your dream may not come in microwave timing, but I promise the timing will be perfect so long as you do your part.

FINISH STRONG

THANK YOU, DREAMER,

This may be the end of the book, but it's just the beginning of the journey for you and your dreams! Now you have more than enough tools to build your dreams on a strong foundation. It's time to stop holding back and show the world who you truly are. It's time to run your race! Release every ounce of fear and doubt and say hello to faith and hope! YOU ARE A BEAST AND NOTHING CAN STOP YOU EXCEPT YOU! Scream it loud!!! "I AM A BEAST AND NOTHING CAN STOP ME BUT ME!!" You're only in competition with yourself, so don't let anyone rush your process. But don't you dare slow down as a safety precaution. All gas and no breaks from here on out!! Your dreams are waiting on you. The graveyard will never see your dreams. I repeat, the graveyard will never see your dreams. Something inside of you has been unlocked and I know you feel it. You have everything you need. So, get up and make it happen!!

Hard times are going to come but you are a survivor. You are not a quitter. You were created to FINISH STRONG! Every dark night will only make you sharper. <u>Embrace your mistakes & believe me when I say they only make you better with time. Keep going and keep growing.</u> If you never quit at your dreams, and you keep growing along the way, eventually you're going to find your sweet spot. There's no doubt about it. So, keep digging because you may be one move away from the biggest moment of your life. You'll never know unless you keep striving. Dreams don't die unless you give up on them and I refuse to let you give up on yours. YOUR TIME IS NOT YESTERDAY OR TOMORROW, IT'S NOW!! This world needs your ideas. We need you to serve the purpose you were created for. YOUR DREAMS MATTER! It's time for you to get out of your own way. Whatever it is, JUST GET UP AND DO IT!

Maybe you've been overlooked or undervalued. It doesn't matter anymore because there are doors waiting to open in your favor! Trust me, if I was able to get you to read my book, then anything in this world is possible including your dreams coming true. The only thing you have to do now is APPLY everything you have learned. Maybe you should read this book twice or even monthly. I would even suggest you writing your favorite parts in a journal or notebook. I don't care what your method is as long as you APPLY the message! There's no more time to waste. Take everything you learned from this book and go create a new game plan because your dreams won't work unless you do! Wait, what's that smell? Oh, I think the dreams are finished cooking. DINGGGG!!! Your MICROWAVE DREAMS are ready to be served. LET'S GET IT DREAM-CHASER!

J. REMY INSPIRES

Jeremy Boykin

INVITE J. REMY INSPIRES
TO SPEAK

EMAIL JREMYINSPIRESBOOKING@GMAIL.COM

Invite Jeremy to your next school, church, or corporate event to experience a life-changing message that you'll never forget.

Jeremy Boykin

Made in the USA
Middletown, DE
23 July 2019